Original title:
A Brooch of Light

Copyright © 2025 Creative Arts Management OÜ
All rights reserved.

Author: Jude Lancaster
ISBN HARDBACK: 978-1-80586-189-8
ISBN PAPERBACK: 978-1-80586-661-9

The Pendant of Hope

In a world of tangled hair,
Hope wears a sparkly flair.
It dangles with a bright grin,
Whispers of joy tucked within.

It's like a bubblegum wish,
Floating on a shiny dish.
Every glance makes hearts do flips,
And giggles dance on playful tips.

Dances of Twilight

Under the moon, shadows prance,
Twilight gives dreams a chance.
They shuffle in mismatched shoes,
Spinning tales of happy blues.

With stars as their clumsy guide,
They wobble, then they glide.
Each twirl leaves a chuckle clear,
In this waltz of night and cheer.

Crystals of Clarity

A crystal ball that won't behave,
Gives saucy insights we crave.
It giggles at our serious plight,
Says, "Dance in your pajamas tonight!"

With every spark, a riddle grows,
Like socks that disappear, who knows?
Yet laughter fills the puzzled air,
As clarity plays hide and seek fair.

Haloed Dreams

Dreams wear halos made of light,
Twinkling jokes that feel just right.
They tickle every sleepy head,
As chuckles dance upon the bed.

With mischief wrapped in starry beams,
They pop like fanciful teams.
Bouncing on clouds of fluffy glee,
They share their secrets joyfully.

Whispers Wrapped in Light

In shadows' dance, a flicker glows,
A giggle sneaks where sunlight flows.
A sparkle lifts the gloomy air,
Like fireflies caught in playful flair.

The sunbeam pokes through cloud's disguise,
As laughter bumbles, joy replies.
With winks and nudges, light will tease,
A secret shared upon the breeze.

The Spark Within

In every heart, a silly spark,
Like firecrackers in the dark.
A chuckle lights the dreary day,
Contentment shines in cheeky play.

With every blink, a twinkle's found,
As giggles bounce and swirl around.
In glowing smiles, let laughter grow,
A hidden gem, a sunny show.

Emblazoned in Luminescence

Through the clouds, a joker beams,
A rainbow spritz of silly dreams.
In beams, we twirl, we leap, we glide,
With silly grins we cannot hide.

Each glow a wink, each shine a tease,
As laughter tumbles with silly ease.
What colors blend in jolly flight,
And tickle us with sheer delight.

Gemstones of Glistening Hope

In a vault of quirky gems,
Laughter sparkles in bright diadems.
Each jest a treasure, a playful cheer,
As joy unfolds, it draws us near.

These bits of shine, oh how they play,
Like mischief on a sunny day.
With giggles twinkling in our eyes,
Hope dances forth in silly guise.

Illuminated Echoes

In a world where shadows play,
Sparkles dance the night away.
A glimmer here, a twinkle there,
Like fireflies without a care.

Glimpses caught in silly poses,
Wiggling like a bunch of roses.
Each flash a laugh, each blink a cheer,
Lightheartedness, we hold so dear.

Ticklish beams and giggling rays,
Shining bright on dreary days.
They flicker jokes in every hue,
Lighting up the skies so blue.

So gather 'round, let laughter flow,
In bright reflections, let joy grow.
For every wink, a chuckle's spun,
A twinkling tale of silly fun!

The Shining Vein

A shimmer caught within a grin,
As silly thoughts are let to spin.
That glint on friends all dressed to play,
With laughter brightening the mundane day.

They trip and twirl in diamond shoes,
Creating light from playful cues.
A shiny hairpin casts a jest,
While light becomes the guest of fest.

In every beam, a tickled tease,
Radiant joy in graceful ease.
Each chuckle shines, a spark of mirth,
Illuminating all our worth.

So shine, my friend, with all your might,
And let your spirit find its flight.
Together we'll dance, a rioting clan,
In a galaxy of beams, oh, how we plan!

Radiance Enshrined

A shimmer of laughter fills the air,
As goofy grins present their flair.
Jokes wrapped tight in silvery glow,
Like butterflies that steal the show.

The lighthearted jokes, they light the dark,
With playful hearts bringing the spark.
They tumble forth in radiant delight,
Chasing away the shadows of night.

We wear our humor as a crown,
With giggles lifting spirits up, not down.
A chandelier of chuckles bright,
Turning mundane scenes into pure delight.

So come and join this silly dance,
Where every glow gives hope a chance.
Together we'll spread this joyful spree,
In a world that shines so endlessly!

Luminary Artifacts

A sparkly bow that bends and weaves,
Around our laughter, it retrieves.
With every snicker, it finds its place,
In the memory of each smiling face.

Bouncy lights reflect our play,
As whimsical thoughts take shape each day.
A giggle twinkling in its flight,
Turns ordinary moments into pure delight.

We'd wear our quirks as shining charms,
In a light that teases and disarms.
Each grin a magic wand we wield,
To bring the light into the field.

So let's adorn this joyous ride,
With beams of laughter as our guide.
His silly spirit shines so bright,
In every heartbeat, find the light!

The Enigma of Brightness

What sparkles in the fridge at night?
A lost snack wearing armor so tight.
Is it cheese or a gem that's slipped away?
Either way, it brings laughter to my day.

A cat with a laser pointer's glee,
Chasing shadows like it's a grand spree.
The sun shines on a tin can's edge,
Creating giggles on every ledge.

Keeper of the Light

In my pocket, a coin shines bright,
I swear it's whispering, 'What a sight!'
Does it think it's a knight in disguise?
Or just a penny with grander lies?

A lamp that flickers, jumps with cheer,
Telling tales of the nighttime deer.
I plug it in, expecting a show,
Instead, the bulb just thinks it's bold!

Cherished Shimmers

Grandma's necklace, a sparkling tale,
Worn by kittens who think they prevail.
Do they pose in the mirror, all glitz and glam?
Or just thinking it's time for a nap, oh, ma'am?

Broccoli crowns that glimmer with might,
Trying to compete with the diamonds so bright.
'We're all stars!' the veggies seem to shout,
'Just with more vitamins; that's what it's about!'

A Cascade of Gleam

A waterfall of glitter, oh what a sight,
Makes my dog think he's flying at night.
With each leap, he sparkles like mad,
Who knew that being silly could make him so glad?

Bubble wrap wrapped in shimmering folds,
A treasure of laughter as it unfolds.
Each pop brings a giggle, a hilarious sound,
In this world of glimmer, joy knows no bound!

A Radiant Charm

In a pocket, a spark does hide,
It tickles my thoughts, here to bide.
A wink from a star, it seems so spry,
'Why not dance?' the little gem cries.

With a flick of my wrist, it takes to flight,
Trailing giggles that dazzle the night.
'Catch me if you can!' it gleefully shouts,
As I chase after joy, skipping about.

Vignettes of Brightness

A glimmer pops out of my old shoe,
It laughs as it rolls, 'I'm shiny, that's true!'
Polishing banter, we giggle and joke,
A beam of pure fun, a luminous poke.

In the fridge, there's a sparkle so spry,
A carrot wearing shades, oh my, oh my!
It winks as I reach, gives my stomach a twist,
Who knew veggies could make such a list?

The Glistening Heart

A pebble of joy, tucked away tight,
With hopes it'll shine like the sun's first light.
Its secret? A tickle, an odd little laugh,
That can turn any sigh into a bubbly craft.

When I wear it at work, people give me a stare,
'What's that glimmer, do we need to beware?'
I smile and reply, 'Just a playful delight,
Making ordinary days a bit more bright!'

Celestial Luminescence

A dust bunny winks from beneath my bed,
With sparkling eyes, it's full of mislead.
'Join me for fun, we'll float up high,'
It laughs as I trip, as I soar and fly.

The moon looks down, it joins in the cheer,
'Let's outshine the stars, let go of the fear!'
With a giggle and wiggle, the darkness retreats,
And we dance with the light on the tips of our feet.

Starlit Charms

In a whimsical night, stars wear their best,
Dancing around, they put light to the test.
With winks and twirls, they giggle and shine,
Each one a charm, a little divine.

Swinging on moonbeams, they play hide and seek,
Tickling the cloud with a giggling cheek.
They're not just glowing, they're plotting some fun,
Under the cosmic, they never outrun.

With a twinkling wink, they jive all night,
They're the party planners of the vast starlight.
Their laughter echoes across the dark veil,
In this cosmic dance, no doubt they prevail.

The Glow Within

There's a light in our hearts that likes to go boom,
Tickled by laughter, it chases the gloom.
It bubbles and giggles like soda pop fizz,
A glow that's contagious, oh what a whiz!

With each silly dance, we stir up the spark,
Our grins shining brightly, lighting the dark.
Like fireflies buzzing, we light up the way,
In this glowing adventure, we're here to play.

So come join the party, don't miss out the chance,
We'll light up the night with our whimsical dance.
In winks and in smiles, we find our delight,
Together we shine, oh what a sight!

Splendor in Stillness

In quiet corners, the lights softly gleam,
Making it cozy, like a sweet little dream.
They chuckle and whisper, as shadows comply,
A serenade of giggles that floats through the sky.

The stillness is a canvas for laughter's display,
With each little sparkle, they dance and they sway.
In silence, they jest, with a magical wink,
A comedy show, if we pause just to think.

From corners of calm, comes a bright little shout,
The stillness is jolly, without any doubt.
So linger a moment, let giggles ignite,
In splendor we shimmer, dazzling the night.

Rays of Enchantment

When the sun dips low, and day turns to night,
Enchanted we are by the magical light.
With laughter like ribbons, they swirl in delight,
These rays of pure mischief, a joyful sight.

Each ray's a little prank, it giggles and teases,
Bouncing off rooftops, catching the breezes.
With playful intentions and mischievous cheer,
They lighten the mood, drawing everyone near.

Oh, rays of enchantment, what fun do you bring?
Riddles and chuckles, like birds on the wing.
In this luminous play, we find our escape,
As laughter and joy paint the night in a cape.

Ethereal Ornaments

In a world where sparkles dance,
A nugget of fun takes its chance.
Jellybeans stuck to a feather's end,
Whispers of laughter with each bend.

A cat in a bow tie struts so proud,
Dressed to impress, he draws a crowd.
Beads of giggles, charms that tease,
Twinkling with mischief, doing as they please.

Glittery shoes that tap on the floor,
Wanna-be stars that search for more.
Wobbling hats that tip and sway,
Turn heads as they parade away.

The universe giggles with bright confetti,
Dancing through moments, oh so petty.
With each twinkle, a story unfolds,
In this light-hearted realm, joy beholds.

Charmed Glow

A chandelier made of candy dear,
Hanging low, it's a treat to appear.
Gummies and chocolates in every light,
Giggling shadows dance out of sight.

A fish in a top hat, quite the sight,
Flipping around like it's a flight.
It splashes with laughs, a nautical show,
Who knew such charm could steal the glow?

Illuminated sneakers, bright and bold,
Running and skipping, never feeling cold.
Frosted cupcakes, twinkling just so,
Each bite's a burst, a delightful glow.

Mirth and chaos in radiant rays,
Lighthearted moments fill all our days.
In every grin and chuckle to share,
Joy blooms brightly, lighting the air.

Luminescent Tokens

A polka dot cat donning a crown,
Chases after dreams while running around.
Wobbling with glee in a shimmer parade,
Spreading sparkles like a playful brigade.

Button-eyed frogs with laughter to lend,
Hop to the rhythm; they know no end.
Chasing the moonlight, a quest they pursue,
With every leap, they gather their crew.

Giggling rainbows in jolly hats,
Grinning at squirrels and chattering cats.
Each twinkle is magic, kind of absurd,
Spreading delight, without a word.

Fluffy clouds puff in a frolicsome spree,
Drifting through dreams, wild and free.
Token of joy in the skies above,
A chase of laughter, a dance of love.

Glowing Reveries

A circus of colors, short and sweet,
Dancing on sidewalks with fairy feet.
Balloons that giggle and swirl like a breeze,
Whispering secrets among the trees.

A muffin that winks with a cherry on top,
Bouncing around like a whimsical flop.
Lemonade rivers flow cheerful and bright,
Sip on the sunshine, a glorious sight.

Noses in books where the unicorns play,
Telling tall tales in the silliest way.
Sparkling giggles pop through the air,
Painting our dreams with whimsy and flair.

Among the stars, a cake made of dreams,
Sprinkled with starlight and moonbeam gleams.
With funky fondants and jellybean tents,
In this frolic, the heart truly repents.

A Tapestry of Flickers

In the closet, old ties hide,
Hoping to be a fashion guide.
One sparkly gem made it through,
Laughing, it shined, what else to do?

A mismatched sock joins the party,
Dancing with flair, oh, so hearty.
Earrings tangled, a curious sight,
Sparkle and giggle, oh what a night!

Balloons float high, swirling in glee,
Bumping a lamp, 'Look at me!'
The cat hops in, with a flick and a flurry,
Then runs off with a brooch, oh what a scurry!

The lamp winks back, quite entertained,
With each little laugh, my heart is gained.
Under this chaos, joy takes flight,
Creating a tapestry in the soft twilight.

Starlit Brooch

A little star on a sweater clasped,
Fell from a sky where fashion's rasped.
It whispered, 'I'm the trendiest light!'
I chuckled, oh what a hilarious sight!

Down the alley, it twinkled bright,
Leading lost socks in a silly flight.
'Where are we going?' asked one with a frown,
To a dance party in a mismatched gown!

Junkyard jewels shone, gleeful and loud,
A diamond ring in a trash can bowed.
'Take a chance!' it said with a wink,
Even the trash has a story, don't think!

Under the moon, everyone swayed,
With sparkle and laughter, unafraid.
This starlit charm, a whimsical spree,
In life's crazy dance, we're all meant to be!

The Glorious Glitter

Glitter bombs burst in laughter's name,
A party of sparkles, all feeling fame.
A rubber chicken clucked at the light,
While disco balls laughed at the sight!

Fridge magnets played musical chairs,
Pasta shells danced without any cares.
'Join us!' they chirped, with gleeful glee,
In this world, even noodles want to be free!

Jelly beans rolled with a comedic jig,
Insisting that candy can dance like a fig.
Oh, we chuckled, with fruits all around,
What glorious glitter our smiles had found!

The cucumber pranced in an ironic tease,
Proclaiming, 'Look at my leafy expertise!'
In this carnival of joy, what a thrill,
Every corner sparkled with gleeful goodwill.

Beacons of the Soul

In a drawer, a mess of laughs do dwell,
Bright buttons inspired, oh can't you tell?
A shoelace twisted in a sly embrace,
Everything sparkles, adding to the ace.

A tiny torch with a smile so wide,
Leading wayward toys on a glittery ride.
'Follow the trail of fun,' it shouts,
Through playful chaos where joy sprout's.

Old comic books flap like crazy birds,
Whispering secrets, exchanging words.
Each turn of a page, a giggle erupts,
In this beacon of joy, love corrupts.

So gather your trinkets, let laughter unfold,
In a world of mischief, memories bold.
These beacons of joy, shining so bright,
Turning every chaos into sheer delight!

Opalescent Tales

Once there was a sparkly gem,
That danced all over whims again.
It slipped upon a dragon's scale,
And bruised the nose of a singing whale.

In sunny skies, it span and twirled,
A polka-dotted whirl, bright and swirled.
It fell into a teapot's brew,
Becoming friends with the sugar, too.

All the knickknacks heard the news,
Of a shiny friend with silly shoes.
They gathered round, and shared a laugh,
As the diamond tried to take a bath.

With every glimmer, tales were spun,
Of offbeat journeys, every pun.
Together in this shiny sphere,
They'd laugh until the stars drew near.

A Dazzling Odyssey

A shiny thing on a grand balloon,
It bounced around, singing a tune.
The clouds giggled as it went by,
Tickling stars in the nighttime sky.

It rode along with a sprightly breeze,
Chasing rainbows with effortless ease.
Once it tumbled down a hill,
And landed on a cat named Jill.

Jill blinked twice, then made a wish,
To swim with fishes in a big dish.
So the sparkle, now quite content,
Turned into shimmer with a tent.

They splashed and played in a sunlit pond,
Creating ripples that grew quite fond.
With every giggle and every beam,
They painted the world like a funny dream.

The Luster of Love

In a jewelry shop with a giddy thrill,
A diamond winked at a tiny quill.
They flirted fiercely, making such glee,
While pearls rolled by, sipping on tea.

The quill twirled, "I write love notes!"
"Let's pen our dreams in giggling coats!"
So off they strode, hand in hand.
Writing silly tales across the land.

With rhymes of cheese and flying cats,
They made the world laugh, even the bats.
The quill would scribble, the gem would glow,
Filling time with a whimsical flow.

In every heart, they'd ignite a spark,
With silly tales to light up the dark.
Together forever, they chirped and shone,
In the sweet embrace where laughter is sown.

Chasing Flickering Dreams

A glimmer flew past a dreaming pup,
It danced in circles, then said, "What's up?"
The pup wagged his tail, gave a bark,
As the light darted near, a teasing spark.

Through fields of daisies, they started to run,
Chasing shadows in the glowing sun.
Each flip and giggle sent butterflies,
Zipping and zooming beneath the skies.

Around a tree, they spun so fast,
Creating memories that were meant to last.
The branches clapped as they skipped with glee,
"Oh, what fun!" said both, "Just you and me!"

With every flicker, dreams took flight,
Waltzing together till the fall of night.
In laughter's embrace, love fully bloomed,
A friendship radiant, forever consumed.

The Shining Mantle

In a world where sparkles play,
The sun wore a coat made of ray.
It sneezed and glitter flew,
Causing birds to say, "Whew!"

The moon, jealous of the bling,
Said, "I need a shiny ring!"
But all she found was dust,
Which made her shimmer rust.

A star tried to join the show,
But tripped on a comet's glow.
It swirled and made a mess,
Creating cosmic stress!

Yet in this chaos we find cheer,
For laughter shines, oh so near!
With silly winks and cheeky beams,
Life's just a series of gleams!

Illuminated Memoirs

Once a lightbulb sparked a tale,
Of how shadows danced like a whale.
It chuckled and giggled bright,
As darkness fled from the sight.

A lamp with a bulb full of dreams,
Shared stories of moonlight beams.
It winked at the walls with glee,
Making them grin wide and free.

The sun joined in on the fun,
Pulling pranks, oh what a run!
It tickled clouds just for kicks,
As rainbows formed in silly flicks.

In every glow and twinkling light,
There's history wrapped up tight.
When laughter mingles with the glow,
Each memory begins to flow!

The Dance of Twinkles

Twinkles had a dance-off spree,
They jiggled and wiggled with glee.
One fell down, a shining flop,
"I shine best from the top!"

Stars formed a conga line,
With giggles that were just divine.
A comet joined in mid-spin,
Saying, "I can twirl and grin!"

The moon tried to join the beat,
But tripped on her own silver feet.
"Who knew this party was so grand?"
As starlight fell upon the land.

In the end, the lights all shone,
Their joyful sparkles brightly grown.
For every slip, a laugh was shared,
In this cosmic jig, all cared!

A Spectrum of Gleams

In a box of colors so bright,
A rainbow sneezed, oh what a sight!
It spilled its hues on the floor,
Making the walls beg for more.

Purple giggled at cheerful red,
While azure blushed and fled.
The yellows danced a jig,
With greens hopping like a pig.

Orange said, "Let's paint the town!"
As the shades twirled round and round.
Each hue had a story to tell,
In this carnival, all was well.

Laughter echoed in every shade,
As colors joined in the parade.
With every gleam and cheeky flare,
Life became a colorful affair!

Flickering Legacy

In the attic, dust and cheer,
Old trinkets dance, they appear.
A tangle of sparkles and sighs,
Whispers of laughter, a surprise.

Grandma's old locket, quite bold,
Once held secrets, now stories told.
It flickers like fireflies in the gloom,
A treasure chest bursting with Zoom!

A hat adorned with odd things found,
Like a disco ball spinning round.
Each charm a giggle, a wink, a nod,
They prance like they've just hit the nod!

So here's to the flickers that stay,
A legacy funny in their own way.
They twinkle and tease, refuse to rest,
In the jewelry box, they're truly blessed.

Adorning the Night

The moon wore diamonds, quite a sight,
While owls hooted, adding delight.
Stars twinkled on a velvet cloak,
The night dressed up, a funny joke!

A crummy old hat tries to steal the show,
But the twinkling lights put on a glow.
Pants of the stars, all faded and torn,
Their laughter bursts, like a brand-new dawn!

The shadows are playing some silly charades,
While comets crash like confetti parades.
The night wears its jewelry, all mismatched and bright,
Adorning the sky, what a hilarious sight!

So let's toast to the glam we can't quite define,
To a night full of laughter and stars that align.
In the cosmic ballet, we twirl and sway,
Wearing the sparkles of night's grand display.

The Luminous Stone

A pebble that glows like a sunbeam smile,
It giggles through puddles, just sits for a while.
Worn by a dog who thinks it's a bone,
Oh, what a funny luminous stone!

It rolls and it bounces, a playful muse,
Chasing the squirrels, spreading the blues.
A treasure to others, a silly delight,
Under the moon, it's a fast furry kite!

Its glow makes the shadows join in the game,
A glowing report card, but no one's to blame.
Itbrightens the path with a good-natured tease,
Even the flowers laugh in the breeze!

So here's to the stone that gives off a grin,
With each little sparkle, it beckons you in.
In the light-hearted romp of this whimsical zone,
Who knew such laughter came from a stone?

Reflections of Dreams

In puddles of starlight, dreams take a dip,
They giggle and shimmer, let's take a quick trip.
Mirrors of laughter bounce off the day,
Reflections of fun in a quirky array!

With each little ripple, a story unfolds,
A cat wearing glasses, a prince made of gold.
Chasing whimsical thoughts through the night,
With echoes of chuckles, it feels so right!

Then comes a turtle, with shades quite divine,
Winking at wishers, in a dance so fine.
Their laughter collides, painting skies bright,
In reflections of dreams, all day and night!

So let's keep the dance of this life in our eyes,
As puddles of dreaming bring laughter that flies.
For in every giggle and shimmering gleam,
Lie the joyous reflections of a beautiful dream!

Beacon of Beauty

In a world so bright and bold,
Where laughter's worth more than gold,
There's a glimmer on my shirt,
Good luck? Or just chocolate dirt?

Like a wink from a cheeky sun,
It makes me feel like I've just won,
With sparkles dancing on my jacket,
Who knew fashion could be a racket?

This shiny thing does steal the show,
But wait, what's that? A bug? Oh no!
It's just a dot, a playful tease,
My treasure bright, my heart at ease.

So wear your gleams with flair and glee,
Let's face the world so whimsically,
A twinkle here, a shimmer there,
Beauty's brooch is everywhere!

Sparkling Echoes

Beneath the skies, so clear and wide,
I flaunt my sparkly joy with pride,
Reflecting giggles, light, and fun,
A fashion statement overdone!

With glitter trails on every hug,
My friends now call me 'Sparkle Bug',
They see my shine, and laugh aloud,
I'm the twinkling centerpiece of the crowd!

As I prance through fields of cheer,
The daisies whisper, 'Hey, come here!'
"Join our disco, dance with flair,
You've got the spark, we love your wear!"

Echoes of laughter fill the air,
As we tumble, toss, with no care,
In sparkly joy, we'll all unite,
For every day's a day of light!

Resplendent Adornments

Oh, look! What's that shining bright?
It's my scarf, or is it a kite?
With sparkly bits that fly and dance,
I'm just trying to brave the glance!

Bedazzled shoes, yet what's the fuss?
They squeak and squawk, oh darling, trust!
Each step I take, a joyful beat,
Fashion's never tasted so sweet!

With every twirl comes a giggle spree,
I'm a merry jester, can't you see?
So let's adorn with colors bright,
Bring joy, and let's not lose the light!

These resplendent things bring smiles galore,
Fashion's laughter? Who could want more?
In this world of fun, let's play,
With sparkly dreams, we'll dance away!

Celestial Accents

Stars twinkle on my feathered hat,
Make it so that I look like that?
An alien queen or just a dream?
Life's much brighter when you beam!

A cosmic giggle from my sleeve,
Adding flair that one can't believe,
With accents from a place so high,
I'm the comet that fell from the sky!

With every twinkling thread and hue,
I'm dressed to sparkle, oh who knew?
Dance in circles, let's have a fight,
In the glow of the moon's soft light.

Celestial sparks will lead the way,
In this funny, whimsical fray,
Let's travel 'round the universe,
With accents that make us converse!

Glimmers of Radiance

In the attic, bins are stacked,
A shiny thing, my heart is racked.
A spoon is bling, a fork's a star,
Who knew cutlery could go so far?

The dog wears jewels, a sparkly crown,
With every wag, it's a shiny gown.
Neighbors chuckle at our parade,
But we shine bright, we're unafraid!

In the garden, weeds dress in lace,
The sunflowers dance in a sunny embrace.
A gnome's got bling, with a retro vibe,
Who knew magic lived in our tribe?

Pinecones drip with glitter and cheer,
We laugh and share in this atmosphere.
In this world where shimmer reigns,
Who needs diamonds when joy contains?

Fragments of Dawn

Morning breaks with a funny twist,
Butterflies wear a fashion list.
Caterpillars strut in tiny shoes,
Who knew they'd have such flashy views?

Roosters crow with a sequined flair,
The cows wear shades, they're quite the pair.
Under the sun, the grass will gleam,
Life's a runway, so chase the dream!

Birds tweet tales of a glamorous flight,
As raindrops sparkle in morning light.
Hopscotch lines made of twinkling dew,
Every leap feels like something new!

With coffee in hand and toast like gold,
Our bustling day begins, so bold.
Fragments of dawn, laughter raised high,
It's a bright new world, oh my, oh my!

Echoes of Shimmer

In a world of giggles, echoes sing,
Old shoes jive, they can really swing.
A cat adorned with a feathered hat,
Sits on a throne, looking quite fat!

Balloons bounce with an elegant flair,
As jellybeans play without a care.
The curtains swirl with a joyful dance,
In a room where laughter takes a chance.

Mustaches made of spaghetti strands,
Ticklish toes and wiggling hands.
A pop of color, oh what a sight,
For in these echoes, we find our light!

With tinsel woven in silly hair,
We strut like peacocks without a care.
Echoes of shimmer, we play and sway,
In the sparkling joy of every day!

Celestial Adornments

Stars wear pajamas made of dreams,
The moon giggles, it often beams.
Winking at planets with silly grace,
Creating a cosmic, joyful space.

Asteroids glide in sequined trails,
With goofy grins, they tell their tales.
Comets dash with candy canes,
In this hilarious dance, joy reigns!

Aliens sport the latest styles,
Shooting moonbeams and goofy smiles.
A starlit party in the night,
Where laughter twinkles, oh what delight!

Galaxies swirl in a bubbly flow,
With celestial bling that steals the show.
Adornments of fun shimmering bright,
We celebrate together, a glorious sight!

Charm of the Ethereal

In the land where shadows play,
A sparkly critter led the way.
It giggled with a wink and cheer,
Whispering secrets in my ear.

I tripped over a rainbow's end,
And made a mess of glitter, my friend.
Dancing on clouds, so fluffy and bright,
Stumbling through day and laughing at night.

A feathered hat upon my head,
Peacocks joined, enough said!
With twirls and jumps, I soared so high,
Pretending I could kiss the sky.

Yet every peek beneath the glow,
Reveals a toe or two on show.
Giggles erupt from the clumsy flight,
As dreams take wing in joyful light.

A Glow Unbound

A jellybean fell from my pocket,
It bounced away like a rocket.
Chasing it down with quite the zest,
I found a dragon in its nest!

With sparkles and snickers, it said,
"Eat more sugar, live without dread!"
I laughed so hard, oh what a sight,
A gummy bear roaring in delight!

Stumbling through fields of cotton candy,
Unearthly creatures danced, so dandy.
Tickled by laughter, I twirled around,
Found cotton clouds on the ground!

With twinkling stars in each pocket worn,
I skipped and hopped, a child reborn.
The universe giggled, oh what a treat,
As I boogied along with candy for feet!

Gleaming Tokens of Time

In a dream with clocks that chime,
Each tick a dance, a quirky rhyme.
The sun wore shades with a laugh so bold,
While time forgot to keep its fold.

I juggled hours like soft balloons,
Each air-filled moment hummed funny tunes.
Tripping on minutes, twirling with glee,
Spinning in circles, oh what a spree!

With wobbly seconds in colorful hats,
I shared my lunch with chittering bats.
They nibbled crumbs with a silly grin,
Tickled by laughter that burst from within.

Time decided to take a break,
And rolled on the grass like a playful snake.
We tangled our joy with a wink and a chime,
Celebrating moments without reason or rhyme.

Light's Intimate Embroidery

A patchwork quilt of giggles so bright,
Stitched together with threads of light.
Each fold a memory, each seam a song,
In this whimsical world where I belong.

Around me, colors burst like cheer,
As fireflies buzzed, whispering near.
They took a bow, and with a gleam,
We danced in moonlight, lost in a dream.

My shoelaces tied by cheerful knots,
Made me dance, forgetting my thoughts.
With every step, a shimmer swirled,
Painting giggles across the world.

With a sprinkle of joy, and laughter to spare,
Light became magic in the air.
We twinkled like stars on a playful spree,
Embroidered in happiness, just you and me.

Adorned in Starlight

When the sun began to snooze,
I wore my lights like glitzy shoes.
Sparkles dance, a playful tease,
Caught on hairdos, sways in breeze.

A wink, a shimmy, a little twirl,
I accessorized my night with a whirl.
Neighbors peeked, stifled a cheer,
My disco ball was born, oh dear!

Crickets chirped with synchronized glee,
As I pranced like a bumblebee.
With each step, I twinkled bright,
Who knew darkness could feel so light?

So let them snicker, let them stare,
My gleaming self doesn't have a care.
When the moon's up, I take my flight,
Adorned in glimmers, what a sight!

Fragments of Radiance

In the pantry, I found some glitz,
A jar of buttons, what a mix!
Each one shines with stories past,
We're all here, having a blast!

I stitched them on my favorite cap,
Now it's a lighthouse—what a map!
A guiding star in grocery lines,
People giggle, say, "What shines?"

Scrambled eggs with sparkles bright,
I cooked breakfast in moonlight.
Salt and pepper in a dance,
Who knew they'd take a chance?

Fragments line up, side by side,
My silly fashion—oh, such pride!
With each step, I strut the floor,
Who knew kitchen wear could score?

Delicate Highlights

In a world of shadows, I frolicked,
A sprinkle here, a dash, it's iconic!
My grandma's pearls, a sight to see,
Who knew they'd shine so playfully?

Dressed like a tree, with fairy lights,
Neighbors term it dazzling sights.
A party in my living room,
Come join the spark, banish gloom!

I juggled spoons from the kitchen rack,
They sparkled bright, no lack to show back.
With each clink, my joy took flight,
In the dull kitchen, a reckless night!

Jazz hands up, let's dance away,
With shimmering dreams, we'll sway and play.
Beneath the fridge, there's laughter loud,
Delicate highlights, we're all so proud!

Emblems of Illumination

Out of the drawer, I pulled a crown,
With bottle caps, I won't back down!
Each emblem gleamed, a festival flair,
Who knew junk could wear such air?

Hats made of paper, buttons galore,
I built an outfit, who could ask for more?
Neighbors whisper, 'Who's that sight?'
I'm their joke, but I feel alright!

Shiny tinfoil wrapped around my wrist,
A disco ball with a silly twist.
Bananas giggle, carrots mock,
In this kitchen, it's pure choc!

Emblems shine, a comic parade,
Instruments of joy that we have made.
So belly laugh and join the fun,
In silly garb, our hearts have won!

Fantasy in Illumination

In the dark, a spark was seen,
A glow from a hat that was quite mean.
It winked at a cat, who looked quite stunned,
And the dog started prancing, oh how he'd run!

A jellybean jumped, and caught the flair,
Dancing on rooftops without a care.
It slipped on a pebble, what a sight to behold,
As the moon just laughed at the tale being told.

Socks started shining, glowing with pride,
While broomsticks laughed, who took them for a ride.
A wizard hiccupped, his wand went ablaze,
As fairies giggled in the moon's gentle haze.

A tuba played tunes that tickled the ground,
Creating a ruckus, oh how they all bound.
In a world where light and laughter collide,
The fun never ended, it was a wild ride.

The Shine We Carry

There's a glow in the pocket, a wink in the shoe,
A bubble of laughter, that's waiting for you.
It tickles the toes and pops like a dream,
Turning all frowns into giggles and gleam.

An umbrella opened, a rainbow went splat,
It flung a few raindrops right at the cat.
The cat wore a frown, then burst into cheer,
As a sunbeam declared, 'Let's dance without fear!'

With glasses that sparkle, and hats that can sing,
Each silly outfit, brings joy like a king.
We prance down the street, with sparkles to share,
As grumpy old neighbors just stop and stare.

Underneath all this fun, a truth we all know,
Together we shine, and together we glow.
In pockets of laughter and dreams ever spry,
A simple reminder, oh my, oh my!

Radiant Chapters

Each turn of the page, a flicker delight,
Words danced off the lines, what a merry sight!
A penguin wore glasses, and schooled with a grin,
While the flamingos tangoed, oh let the fun begin!

The knight lost his horse to a game of charades,
As dragons played hopscotch, in hilarious shades.
A princess in pajamas danced with a broom,
While the storybook laughed, spilling joy through the room.

A cake made of jelly, with candles that winked,
Sang songs of adventure, with sprinkles of pink.
As laughter filled taverns, and echoed through halls,
Each radiant chapter, invited us all.

So gather your friends, with giggles and cheer,
For the tales that we tell are the ones we hold dear.
In a world full of wonders and bright, sparkling loads,
The chapters of laughter light up all our roads.

A Light Unchained

A light bulb rebelled, it refused to obey,
It bounced on a table, and started to play.
With quirks and flashes, it sparked quite a scene,
As chairs started dancing, like they were on scene.

Candles began giggling, their flames took a prance,
They twirled in the air, pulled into a dance.
A shadow ran for cover, all startled and shy,
While the laughter exploded, like popcorn on high.

A squirrel with a flashlight turned things upside down,
Chasing beams of light all around the town.
A crowd gathered 'round, hats all in a whirl,
As a spark could ignite both a laugh and a twirl.

In this whimsical space where silliness reigns,
We find every giggle, in the light that remains.
So cherish these moments, let humor proclaim,
A light unchained is the heart of our game.

Shines of Enchantment

In the wild, a spark did gleam,
A squirrel paused, began to scheme.
It wore a hat of shiny foil,
And danced on grass with graceful toil.

The sun peeked out, a wink so sly,
As rabbits dressed began to fly.
A gleeful parade of glowing things,
With sparkly bows and feathered wings.

In the midst of laughter, jewels did collide,
Ducks donned tiaras, they couldn't hide.
Each twinkle snorted, filled with cheer,
For who knew laughter sparkled here?

So let us take a moment bright,
To cherish sparkles through the night.
For in this whimsy, we find delight,
And dance with joy in pure delight.

Moonlit Keepsakes

Under the stars, a glow did twirl,
With fireflies buzzing, the night did whirl.
A raccoon strutted, beads in tow,
In a shiny cloak, stealing the show.

The moon grinned down, a silver ball,
While frogs in tuxedos began to crawl.
Each leap was met with a joyful cheer,
As crickets chirped, "The end is near!"

A treasure hunt for gleams and shimmers,
While playful shadows waltzed with glimmers.
With twinkling eyes, we joined the fight,
To chase the charm that danced with light.

So gather round, dear friends, behold,
The tales of laughter, we retold.
In moonlit moments, smiles ignite,
And all our worries take to flight.

Glint of Dreams

In the garden, visions bloom,
With whirls of colors, banishing gloom.
A gnome, with flair, wore shades of jade,
Comme une rockstar, he bravely played.

A ladybug in sequins bright,
Swayed to the rhythm, a pure delight.
With sparkly sneakers, it started to break,
The very ground with a tiny quake.

The stars chuckled, their laughter shared,
As more whimsy danced, as if unprepared.
With each gleam, a funny twist,
In the dreamland, how could we resist?

So prance about, with mirthful screams,
In this world of sparkly dreams.
Where quirks abound and joys redeem,
And laughter's light is supreme.

Radiant Tokens of Affection

With ribbons bright, the lovers met,
Under the moon, they placed their bet.
A wink, a smile, a cheeky tease,
As butterflies danced on the evening breeze.

So what if squirrels wear fancied hats?
And owls are painting with splashes of spat,
The glow of laughter wrapped them tight,
With each token holding pure delight.

Laughter echoed under the stars,
As frogs played tunes on their shiny guitars.
Each silly moment, a cherished score,
In their hearts, they'd implore for more.

So gather your joys, shine brightly and sing,
For each little moment is a charming thing.
In a world of glimmers, may laughter stay,
And brighten our journeys, come what may.

Auroral Elegance

A dainty spark in morning's glow,
Slipped from a cloud, just to say hello.
Dancing on pins like a jittery spree,
What a sight for you and me!

Twinkling like stars on a chilly night,
It wobbles and jiggles, oh what a sight!
It may look fancy, but not too bright,
Like a chaotic peacock, oh what a fright!

Wrapped in laughter, glints and gleams,
Crafty little trinket of joyous dreams.
Frolicking gaily with mischief and style,
A whirling dervish, guaranteed to beguile!

In every pocket and purse it may land,
Daring the world to join its grand stand.
With a wink of the eye and a twirl of the wrist,
Oh, the fun that we surely can't miss!

Gemstones of the Soul

Glittering pebbles from a fairy tale,
They sing and they dance, telling their tale.
Off to the market, they bounce with glee,
As shoppers gaze rapt with bewilderment, see!

Emerald giggles and sapphire sighs,
Chasing the pigeons up in the skies.
Raucous adventures in a world so bright,
Each gemstone whispers, 'Come join the invite!'

In coffee cups, they conspire and scheme,
Planning a heist of the next ice cream.
Wrapped in humor and fashioned in fun,
It's a riotous world when their day's just begun!

With every shimmer, they tickle the air,
Sprinkling laughter like they just don't care.
In the zany world of gem lore galore,
Who needs the ordinary? We want more!

The Ethereal Spark

A flicker of whimsy, bright and spry,
Glistening secrets in the blink of an eye.
Dancing in shadows, oh what a tease,
They giggle and wiggle, like playful bees!

With the charm of a cat and a twist of fate,
They soar through the air, but never too straight.
Popping like bubbles in hazy delight,
Bringing us joy with their radiant flight!

They tickle the edges of countless smiles,
Spreading their magic across many miles.
With a hint of the silly and dash of grace,
Each little spark lights up every place!

In the realm of the quirky and silly and bright,
We find our joy, oh what a sight!
Forever they play, with laughter so stark,
These cheeky little fellows—the ethereal spark!

Prism of Possibilities

Colors collide in a whimsical show,
A jester's parade, oh how they glow!
Each hue is a giggle, each shade is a cheer,
Painted in laughter, let's all draw near!

Twisting like vines in a garden so rare,
They frolic in sunshine, just stop and stare.
Frivolous rays do a cheeky dance,
Wrapping us up in a joyful trance!

With every flicker a new chance to play,
An invitation to the silliest day.
Think outside the box, let imagination roam,
In this kaleidoscope, you're always at home!

Blending in colors, from shy to brash,
In laughter we bask, in whimsy we splash.
The world is our canvas, so let's not delay,
Let's leap into brilliance, come join the ballet!

Shards of Illumination

In a pocket, lost socks giggle,
They shine brighter than a baby's wiggle.
A cat sat on a sunbeam's flair,
It thought it was a purr-fect chair.

A pickle jar glows in the frost,
Confetti of dreams, not a moment lost.
The light bulbs dance with electric glee,
Whispering secrets of a buzzing bee.

Stray dog in shades, strutting with pride,
Under disco balls, he takes a ride.
Each glow a giggle, a chuckle so bright,
Who knew this world could be such a sight?

A glowworm ballroom in the evening tide,
Worms in tuxedos, they break their stride.
Jellybeans bounce in a sugary groove,
Their silly disco steps make you move.

Twilight's Adornment

In twilight's pastel, a goat wears a crown,
With sunglasses on, he struts through the town.
Fireflies buzz like they own the night,
Each one a lamp with a blink so bright.

A raccoon in a tutu, swaying with flair,
Dancing on rooftops, without a care.
Stars giggle loudly, a celestial horde,
As the moon takes notes, with an eager hoard.

The shadows play tag, it's quite the scene,
A squirrel steals acorns, all glimmer and glean.
When daylight retreats, silly antics ignite,
In this twilight garden, everything's right.

A snail in a spotlight, taking its time,
With glittery trails, it's a slow dance rhyme.
Each glint a cheer, each glimmer a joke,
This nighttime party, not a whispered poke.

A Symphony of Light

A saxophone glow from a nearby tree,
Funky tunes spill out like a jubilant spree.
Fireflies groove, swaying side to side,
Making sweet music where shadows abide.

A goldfish in glasses, so chill and so cool,
Swims like a champ in a watery pool.
The turtles are clapping, they're feeling the beat,
In their conga line dance, they shuffle their feet.

Stars join the chorus, they wink and they prance,
Dropping down notes, sparking up a romance.
A rabbit on drums, thumping with glee,
While the chorus of crickets hums harmony.

Lollipops flash in a wild disco ball,
As gummy bears waltz, having a ball.
This radiant jamboree, aflame and bright,
Who knew that joy could shine with such light?

Embraced by Luminescence

In the glow of the fridge, leftovers play,
They twirl and they wiggle in a fridge ballet.
Ketchup and mustard, a condiment fight,
Battling it out in the soft glowing light.

A toaster's toast has a knack for flair,
Launching its bread like it's flying through air.
Jam jars in taffeta, sparkly delight,
Start their own dance in the quiet of night.

Doughnuts wear sunglasses, sassy and round,
Rolling through kitchens, making a sound.
A giggle from cupcakes, icing so bright,
Their sprinkles are shining, pure joy in flight.

On the windowsill, a plant holds a chat,
With a lamp post who rocks a sweet little hat.
In this world of brightness, each giggle ascends,
As the night sheds its worries and laughter blends.

Glimmers of Grace

In a dress that sparkles bright,
Old Uncle Joe claims it's just right.
He wears it with a smile so wide,
Saying fashion's a joyful ride.

The cat thinks it's a toy to chase,
Dancing around with feline grace.
While Auntie laughs at the sight so fun,
"What a show!", she says, "You're the crazy one!"

A rhinestone fell from high above,
Landed on Dad, who swore it was love.
He struts and poses like a star,
Says he'll make it to Hollywood, or at least the bar!

With every twinkle, laughter flows,
In our clumsy dance, everyone knows.
Life's little quirks, our hearts embrace,
In this joyful chaos, we find our place.

The Shimmering Emblem

A badge of honor, or so it seems,
Worn by Greg, lost in daydreams.
He thinks it adds to his charm,
But it's really just a shiny harm.

At dinner, it falls into the stew,
"Oh dear!" he shouts, "What should I do?"
Everyone giggles, the spoons take flight,
"Let's dig in!" they cheer, "What a sight!"

The dog licks it, making it shine,
Greg shrugs, "I'll wear it, it's truly divine!"
As it gleams and winks in delight,
He says, "Fashion rules are out of sight!"

But when the night comes to an end,
It's the laughter we cherish, the joy we send.
In every glimmer, absurd and bright,
The shimmering emblem brings us light.

Illuminated Keepsake

A trinket found in Granny's chest,
Shiny and odd, it's quite the jest.
She claims it's magic, a family key,
To open laughs and joy, you see!

On a hike, it flips right off her coat,
"Oops!" she yells, as around it floats.
The squirrels gather, all eyes on the glint,
"We've struck gold!" they squeak, "In a tiny print!"

A dance-off starts beneath the trees,
As creatures gather, swaying in the breeze.
Grandad's in a tutu, doing his thing,
With every wiggle, this keepsake will sing.

In the chill of night, we all unite,
To share our stories under the moonlight.
With every sparkle, old tales awake,
Laughter rings out, in this keepsake's wake.

Dazzle in the Darkness

A glow-in-the-dark pin on my chest,
Shines so bright, I'm truly blessed.
But in a blackout, what a surprise,
My dance moves make others roll their eyes.

I twirl and jiggle, the floor is my stage,
Using my light, I unplug the rage.
Neighbors peek out, wonders unfold,
"Is that a disco?" the stories are told.

In shadows we shine, no need for pomp,
Just silly shapes as we twist and romp.
I trip on my shoelace, stumble and fall,
Yet the laughter that follows astounds us all.

We dazzle together, in this light-hearted spree,
Underneath the stars, we're perfectly free.
In every giggle, in every spark,
We find our joy and lighten the dark.

Opalescent Murmurs

In the garden of quirks, they unfold,
Mirth shines like gems, stories retold.
Dancing daisies in sunny delight,
Whispering secrets under moonlight.

Bumblebees bumbling, they trip in the air,
Sticky with nectar, without a care.
Laughter erupts, as they buzz all around,
Nature's own jesters, so joyfully found.

Caterpillars wearing a wig made of grass,
Trying to fit in with a giggling class.
They twirl and they twist, but never quite sway,
In this wacky world, they dance and they play.

So here's to the chaos that makes us all smile,
A flicker of fun, make it last for a while.
Hold on to the silliness, let spirits ignite,
With opalescent murmurs, everything's bright!

The Radiant Embrace

In a sweater that's bright, with spots and some stripes,
Frogs hop on a pogo, embracing their types.
With giggly green hats and shoes that squeak loud,
They jump in the air, proud and unbowed.

The sun winks at squirrels, tossing acorns with glee,
As stories of cheese roll around, just for free.
A turtle slow dances, its rhythm quite slick,
While rabbits start laughing, they're pacing too quick.

Clouds shaped like ice cream swirl high in the sky,
Tickling the sunbeams that wink as they fly.
Oh, to be part of this radiant race,
Where joy rolls in laughter and moments embrace.

Hold tight to your laughter, let it spin and sway,
In this whimsical dance, let worries decay.
The beauty of nonsense, a warm, goofy grace,
With a radiant embrace, we all find our place!

Dawn's Secret Treasures

Upon the rising sun, a secret at play,
Gnomes take to the streets in a funny ballet.
With boots made of clovers, they prance and they twirl,
Spinning yarns of dreams, giving life a great whirl.

In the cool morning mist, a riddle does leap,
When chickens tell tales, it's laughter they reap.
They cluck in a chorus, each note quite absurd,
Reciting their tales in a flurry of words.

The hedgehogs with tiaras, as regal as crowns,
Lead parades through the flowers, with fluttering gowns.
Oh, dawn's secret treasure, a tapestry bright,
Where witty little critters spread pure delight.

So gather the giggles, hold them close, let them sing,
For in every small moment, joy springs.
With dawn's secret treasures, let laughter take flight,
In the embrace of the day, everything feels right!

Flickers of the Heart

A pickle wearing glasses, reading a tale,
In a world made of jelly, we both set sail.
With marshmallows giggling, oh what a sight,
Flickering laughter, our spirits take flight.

Jumping jellybeans dance on a plate,
Inviting the day with a joyful gait.
They rattle and shake, a colorful crew,
Making mischief in ways that are quite new.

Between the bursts of joy, there's a spark,
As kazoos serenade while playing in the park.
A note from a taco, wrapped tight with cheer,
Says life tastes much better with friends always near.

So let's keep on smiling, through thick and through thin,
With every little giggle, new adventures begin.
In those flickers of the heart, we find our own part,
And share in the essence of joy from the start!

A Veil of Illumination

In the shade, a glow appears,
A twist of fate that cheers our peers.
With sparkles dancing up the stairs,
Who's got the light? We'll play the bears!

A feathered cap, a bright disguise,
With every step, it's sure to surprise.
A wink, a nudge, who needs to try?
When laughter's the goal, we'll never die!

The moon peeks in; we tell a joke,
A wobbly chair and then we croak.
No serious vibe, just silly glee,
Existence is rough; let's have some tea!

So gather 'round for this delight,
The glow we've found is pure and bright.
With each laugh shared, the world spins round,
In this glowing veil, joy can be found.

Reflections of Grace

In every mirror, a silly face,
Grins in the glass, we're full of grace.
We flip our hair, strike poses bold,
Then laugh until our sides are rolled.

A wiggly dance in sparkling shoes,
Twirl like a whirlwind—we won't lose!
Who needs the floor? Let's just float,
On bubbles made of dreams, we'll gloat.

With each thin slice of shining pie,
We toast to life, no need to cry.
The best reflections bring out the glee,
So let's delight in pure jubilee!

Each wink and giggle creates a space,
Where joy stands tall, a bright embrace.
In every heart, these echoes trace,
The sweetest song of love's embrace.

The Glittering Path

On a trail of sparkles we will sashay,
Side by side, let's boogie away.
With every step, giggles ignite,
As we dance under stars tonight.

A shiny rock? Oh, what a find!
A treasure chest for the silly-minded.
Each shiny object tells a tale,
Of mischief-making without fail!

Through bushes thick, we chase the gleam,
A path of laughter, a joyful dream.
In this wild journey, hearts so light,
We leave behind shadows of fright.

So follow the glimmer, don't be slow,
Let the bright laughter steal the show.
With every glow, the world feels bright,
On this glittering path, joy takes flight!

Gleaming Threads of Destiny

We're weaving tales with shiny threads,
Silly patterns dance in our heads.
With knots of laughter, tightly spun,
In this fabric, the fun's begun!

Each stitch we make adds to the glow,
Crazy colors in the show.
With every loop, a giggle grows,
A tapestry where craziness flows.

In puffy hearts, these threads reside,
A patchwork quilt we'll wear with pride.
Let's stitch the night with twinkling cheer,
In this crazy world, we shed a tear!

All tangled up in joy's embrace,
We'll pull the seams, the best of grace.
With gleaming threads, our souls will fly,
In this fun design, we won't say goodbye!

www.ingramcontent.com/pod-product-compliance
Lightning Source LLC
Chambersburg PA
CBHW060135230426
43661CB00003B/433